Tarot Cards for Beginners

A Beginner's Guide to Learning Tarot Card Reading, Meanings, & Spreads

Text Copyright © Lightbulb Publishing

All rights reserved. No part of this guide may be reproduced in any form without permission in writing from the publisher except in the case of brief quotations embodied in critical articles or reviews.

Legal & Disclaimer

The information contained in this book and its contents is not designed to replace or take the place of any form of medical or professional advice; and is not meant to replace the need for independent medical, financial, legal or other professional advice or services, as may be required. The content and information in this book has been provided for educational and entertainment purposes only.

The content and information contained in this book has been compiled from sources deemed reliable, and it is accurate to the best of the Author's knowledge, information, and belief. However, the Author cannot guarantee its accuracy and validity and cannot be held liable for any errors and/or omissions. Further, changes are periodically made to this book as and when needed. Where appropriate and/or necessary, you must consult a professional (including but not limited to your doctor, attorney, financial advisor or such other professional advisor) before using any of the suggested remedies, techniques, or information in this book.

Upon using the contents and information contained in this book, you agree to hold harmless the Author from and against any damages, costs, and expenses, including any legal fees potentially resulting from the application of any of the information provided by this book. This disclaimer applies to any loss, damages or injury caused by the use and application, whether directly or indirectly, of any advice or information presented, whether for breach of contract, tort, negligence, personal injury, criminal intent, or under any other cause of action.

You agree to accept all risks of using the information presented in this book.

You agree that by continuing to read this book, where appropriate and/or necessary, you shall consult a professional (including but not limited to your doctor, attorney, or financial advisor or such other advisor as needed) before using any of the suggested remedies, techniques, or information in this book.

Table of Contents

Chapter 1: Introduction 1

Chapter 2: How to Get Started 5

Chapter 3: Reading the Cards Daily 7

Chapter 4: Card Interpretations - The Major Arcana 11

    0. The Fool. 12

    I. The Magician. 13

    II. The High Priestess. 14

    III. The Empress. 15

    IV. The Emperor. 16

    V. The Hierophant. 17

    VI. The Lovers. 18

    VII. The Chariot. 19

    VIII. Strength. 20

    IX. The Hermit. 21

    X. Wheel Of Fortune. 22

    XI. Justice. 23

    XII. The Hanged Man. 24

    XIII. Death. 25

    XIV. Temperence. 26

    XV. The Devil. 27

    XVI. The Tower. 28

    XVII. The Star. 29

    XVIII. The Moon. 30

XIX. The Sun..31

XX. Judgement..32

XXI. The World...33

Chapter 5: Card Interpretations - The Minor Arcana.........................35

Swords...35

Wands 50

Cups 64

Pentacles 78

Chapter 6: Tarot Spreads...93

Chapter 7: Creating your Tarot Space 97

Chapter 8: Conclusion 99

Chapter 1
Introduction

The tarot can be full of surprises, just like the time I won a free reading many years ago. That was how I was introduced to the tarot and it led me to the exciting journey of exploring the cards for myself. How wonderful that you've taken an interest in learning about them too! Having your own deck of cards and learning how to relate to them can be a soul-enriching process.

The tarot is a mirror into the soul's journey of realizing itself in the world, and anyone who uses it has the opportunity to look deeply into this mirror as it reflects their own inner processes back to them. Just like any new journey, we do not quite know what is in store for us yet, but with an open mind and a good dose of curiosity, this journey can be fun and nourishing.

When I got my first tarot deck, I was excited and a bit overwhelmed at how much there was to learn. Thanks to friends and many good resources I found my way quickly. Getting to know your cards can be a fun process as I hope you will soon discover. Of course, there may be times of uncertainty. You may wonder if you're "doing it right" or if you're intuitive enough, but if you can let these thoughts pass, you will begin to enjoy a deeper level of connection to your cards. As with any skill, practice goes a long way toward becoming a great reader.

The tarot can be used in many ways: for magic, fortune-telling, divination, and as a tool for psychological exploration and self-development. I use the cards as a tool for personal growth and self-understanding and this book will reflect that. The tarot helps me work with the **here and now.** I prefer not to do readings to predict the future. In my view, doing so limits the infinite possibilities of the present. Of course, while consulting the cards, we can see patterns develop, and explore what actions could lead to various outcomes in a rational way. But in no way are these fixed.

In acknowledging our own agency and capacity to change a situation, we take responsibility for our lives. We can dive deeper into our motivations and intentions rather than leave it up to destiny. As empowered human beings with the capacity to learn from our surroundings and make conscious decisions, we have the power to make our lives and the lives of those around us better. Exercising this capacity to pause, consider, reflect and proceed is a great power the tarot can support us in wielding.

Before we proceed, take a moment to reflect on the following questions:

What brings you to the tarot?

What are you inspired by?

What is Tarot?

The tarot is a deck of 78 cards, divided into two sets known as the Major and the Minor Arcana. These cards have been used for centuries for various purposes—card games being one of the earliest known uses. This book illustrates the use of the cards for Tarot readings.

The word Arcana means profound secret or mystery. As we will discover while further exploring the cards, the Major Arcana contain many important themes and stories that unfold in our lives and the Minor Arcana depict the more mundane happenings or minor themes of our lives. It is important to note that the Minor Arcana are in no way less important than the Major Arcana; it is important to have a reading that not only highlights the big picture but also allows us to examine the intricate details of the subject at hand, allowing us to deepen our understanding of the Self and its workings.

The Major Arcana consist of 22 cards starting with 0 (The Fool) and ending with 21 (The World). The Minor Arcana consist of 56 cards and are divided into four suits: Swords, Wands, Cups and Pentacles. In each suit there are 10 'pip' cards numbered Ace to Ten and four 'face' or 'court' cards depicting a Page, a Knight, a Queen and a King.

The beginner tarot enthusiast may become overwhelmed by the detail in each of these cards, but with practice, one becomes familiar with the patterns, the relationships between the cards, and the story that unfolds through and across the Arcana, the suits and the entire deck. Therefore, it is advised to stay open and curious and allow the tarot to tell you its story as you progress in your journey with it.

History of the Tarot

The origins of the tarot are largely unknown. The cards first appeared in Europe as playing cards in the 14th century and have been found in parts of Italy and France where artists were commissioned by nobility to paint handmade and customized cards featuring members of the noble families in the trump or Major Arcana cards. Some claim that the original cards came from Egypt;

others link the cards to Jewish Kabbalah. It is said that the cards have also been found in ancient China, linking it to the I-Ching, and some even claim they're connected to India through Tantra. Many cards have been found across the world with similarities, so there is no consensus on where the original tarot came from. Even the etymology of the word 'taro' is unknown. Some believe it to be Egyptian, others link it to the Torah in Hebrew, and others still claim it to be Latin. Despite their unknown origins, the cards found widespread acclaim and have lived on beyond their early use as playing cards. Occultists, gypsies and magicians began using them as tools for divination, fortune telling and character reading, and the cards have survived centuries of changes. Though altered and influenced profoundly over the ages, the cards have managed to keep their basic structure intact to this day.

Chapter 2
How to Get Started

Choosing a Tarot Deck

If you're wondering which deck is right for you, the simplest answer is to pick the one you feel most drawn to. There are many tarot decks out there and there might be one deck to suit every kind of person.

I began reading the tarot with the Rider-Waite deck. This is a classic deck of cards that you can't go wrong with. There are many Rider-Waite inspired decks that keep the same general visuals while adding a theme. Decks like those are also okay for a beginner reader. The best thing about these cards is that they are simple to read; the pictures are self-descriptive and evoke some impressions that you can work with right away without having to memorize the traditional meanings. The deck's original illustrator, Pamela Coleman Smith, painted human characters for most of the Minor Arcana cards, apart from the trump cards, which helps readers draw meaning from the cards based on the depictions. This is certainly easier than seeing a card with, for example, six wands or two cups and trying to interpret it.

Two other popular decks are the Tarot of Marseilles and Aleister Crowley's Thoth deck. In this book, I stick to the Rider-Waite cards and all the exercises and interpretations are based on this deck. The interpretations are universal, so if you have a different deck, do not fret; you'll quickly learn how to make it work for you and tune into your intuition and storytelling skills based on what you read here.

Try to keep your decision simple. As many tarot readers will tell you, you may choose to have more than one deck as you progress in your journey with the tarot, and you will turn to certain decks based on what kind of reading you are doing and how you connect with each of your decks.

Tarot Journal

The other tool I highly recommend for beginners is their own tarot journal. Having a dedicated journal for your tarot readings is a great way to learn more about your cards and yourself. By recording your readings and reflections in your journal you can revisit earlier experiences with the tarot and see how your journey has developed. As your perspective widens, you can keep adding to your treasure chest of tarot wisdom and relish in the richness of what you are creating for yourself!

Connecting with Your Cards

It's time to get started. If you haven't already done so, unpack your deck. Here's a little exercise to introduce yourself to the cards and bond with them:

Hold the deck in your hands. Close your eyes and become aware of your breath. Ground your energy into the earth. Call on your inner guidance to have a non-verbal conversation with the cards and put your best intentions into them. Open your eyes and begin to examine the cards. Give them a little shuffle and briefly look through each of the 78 cards. Allow whatever comes to you effortlessly to land in your subconscious mind as you observe the images, colors, characters, symbols and scenes depicted.

Chapter 3
Reading the Cards Daily

Now that you have connected with your cards, it's time to familiarize yourself with them. The best way to do this is to read. For beginners, I always recommend you start by simply **reading for yourself**. You may have friends who are excited and want a reading from you right away, but the best thing to do at this point is to politely turn down these requests and let them know you're just learning to do this for yourself and perhaps in the near future you will be open to reading for friends and family. By learning to read for yourself, you begin to develop a close relationship with your cards without any external pressure. You can begin practicing right away and there is no need to know everything about the cards or the traditional meanings assigned to them before you read.

When you come to the tarot with a question, you might be looking for one answer or you might be interested in a more detailed view. There are many possible combinations or layouts which can provide you with what you need. These layouts in the tarot are called **spreads**. Many spreads have been created and recorded through the history of tarot. There is one that even uses all 78 cards; imagine that! In this book we will stick to a few simple spreads and I will walk you through a few exercises so you can begin doing readings right away.

Before you begin a reading, prepare your space. Skim through Chapter 7 on creating a tarot space. This is something that will evolve with your practice. As a beginner, you can start by finding a spot in your house where you feel drawn to work with the cards. A meditation cushion or any simple, uncluttered space will do.

In this chapter, we will do a one-card reading to get you started; I will detail more spreads in Chapter 6. I recommend doing the one-card and two-card spreads for at least 15 days before you move on to the others. Keep it as simple as possible in the beginning to find your flow with the readings. Once you develop your skills, you'll be confident enough to read more complex spreads.

One-Card Reading

A one-card reading is a great way to get to know your cards. You can do this daily, perhaps in the morning or at bedtime as an awareness tool. This reading is also used for 'yes or no' questions, decision making, and for making a quick assessment of a situation.

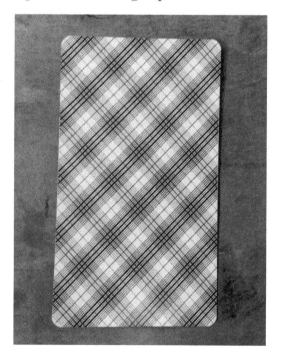

Preparatory Meditation:

Find a quiet seat. Close your eyes. Sense the contact your body is making with the floor and observe how you feel here. Notice your spine and allow it to be soft and supported. Now bring your awareness and acceptance to your breath and let the body soften and receive the ease that pours into you through each breath. Take five breaths with conscious awareness.

Begin by shuffling your cards and as you do, think of the question or concern you have that you would like to do a reading for. By shuffling as you consider this, you are exchanging energy with the cards. Note: This is the same process you will use when you begin to read for others - you will shuffle your cards as they connect with their query and share it with you.

Once you are ready, cut the cards (divide them) into three stacks to the left and once again stack them all together in no particular order. Continue this process of shuffling and cutting until you feel ready.

Then pick out the top card on the pile.

Observe your immediate reactions and responses as you see this card. *What does the scene depict? What words would you use to describe the scene? What character(s) in the scene are you most drawn to? How does this card relate to your situation? Does this remind you of something or someone in your life? What emotions do you feel as you take in the colors in the card? Do you feel open to this card? What resistance do you meet in yourself, if any? What can you learn from this card today?*

Enter your responses into your tarot journal. You can use the format below:

Date and Time	
Query	
Card	
Keywords, Observations, Feelings, Thoughts	
Additional Comments	

Once this process is complete, offer silent gratitude to the cards and all who supported you in your practice. Place the card back in the deck and shuffle or keep the card with you or on your desk to view as you go about the rest of your day. You can return the card to the deck at the end of the day. You can also return to your journal entry at the end of the day or on a later date to see what has emerged from the situation since then and how the process worked for you. Add comments from your current perspective.

Practicing the one-card reading every day is a great way to get to know your cards better.

In Chapters 4 and 5, we'll learn about the traditional interpretations of the Major and Minor Arcana. You can refer to these meanings during your readings or whenever you feel the need to. Many schools of tarot ascribe different meanings to the cards. The interpretations in this book are based on my personal experience and influenced by the many resources I have learned from over the years. As you develop your own practice, you should rely less on these interpretations and more on your own wisdom, creativity and intuition, and form a vocabulary of your own that reflects your unique essence as a tarot reader.

Chapter 4
Card Interpretations - The Major Arcana

We begin with the Major Arcana - a set of 22 cards, from 0 (the Fool) to 21 (the World). This represents the Fool's journey through the Major Arcana, revealing profound secrets every step of the way. At each step, the Fool, representing the soul birthed into physical existence, meets an archetype of the human experience, and from each one the Fool learns something new and expands his awareness to accommodate a larger Self. These cards are also known as trump cards, and they reveal the larger themes in one's life.

0. THE FOOL.

The white sun shines in the sky as the Fool embarks on a journey, open chested and unguarded, throwing caution to the wind and carrying a few belongings in a sack tied to the end of a stick which rests lightly on his right shoulder. In his left hand, he carries white flowers, the color white symbolizing purity. The feather in his cap symbolizes truth. With a landscape of ice-capped mountains in the background, he seems to be walking close to the edge of a cliff with a carefree or perhaps unaware attitude. A white dog by his feet seems to be an ally to this curious man and is perhaps warning him of the dangers that lie ahead.

When the Fool's energy shows up in your life, you could be at the beginning of a profound process or journey. You find yourself drawn to the mystery. Unaware of what in you is drawn to this energy, you lean into a childlike self that is open and trusting of messages from the outside. You are eager to learn from what lies ahead.

I. THE MAGICIAN.

The young magician in this picture is infused with life force represented by the yellow background. His white wand aimed at the skies represents purity in intent. Almost posed like a lightning rod, he stands in openness, directing Spirit from the Universe to move through him and grounding it into the Earth as he points downwards with his left hand. The red robe signifies his spirituality and compassion. He stands behind a table of intentions representing the four suits of the tarot - the pentacle (earth), cup (water), wand (fire) and sword (air). He is ready to manifest Spirit into Matter as he stands in a garden of red roses and white lilies. The red roses symbolize personal desires and white lilies symbolize universal laws. An infinity sign looms above his head, signifying the flowing potential of the Magician. The Fool meets the Magician and is now armed with all the tools (elements or suits) that he needs to continue his journey.

"As above, so below."

When you get this card in a reading, you are ready to act. You are being shown that you already have the potential to take up the project or journey that presents itself to you. You are now in a position to manifest something and you can tap into Source energy to bring your dreams into reality on the physical plane. Nothing has manifested yet, but you have gathered your tools at this stage.

II. THE HIGH PRIESTESS.

The High Priestess sits on a throne in the doorway to the Temple of Solomon between two pillars: white (Jakin) and black (Boaz), which represent the active and passive aspects of the imagination. She holds a partially concealed scroll in her lap and wears blue and white robes with the new moon at her feet. She wears a lunar crown on her head which represents emotional changes. She is the keeper of the records. She holds secret wisdom and represents intuition and inner knowing. The Fool begins to make his own journey inwards.

The High Priestess is the unmanifested potential in you that is waiting to be activated. It is the energy that inspires you to look deep within. It teaches you to tap into your own inner guidance. Trust in your intuition, emotions and feminine knowing; they are here to guide you through the unconscious mysteries of your own being.

III. THE EMPRESS.

Now the Fool meets the Empress, known as the Mother card, seated on a soft pillow. She wears a full flowing gown and a crown of stars. She is perhaps pregnant. She holds a crystal wand in her right hand. Below her rests a shield with the sign of Venus, symbolizing loving protection. The trees and wheat surrounding her signify nature and abundance. The flowing stream signifies the 'River of Life' and the nourishment of feelings.

This is the card of creation. When you get this card, you are ready to bring something into physical existence. You are pregnant with an idea that is about to come to fruition. This is also a card of self-nurturing, care and healing. It points to our primary connection with the Mother Earth.

IV. THE EMPEROR.

The Emperor is considered the Father in the Major Arcana. He sits in a calm and relaxed seated position and radiates authority and confidence. The rams on his throne represent Aries, ruler of the head. The Emperor's hair and beard are white, symbolizing ancient wisdom. He holds a scepter in his right hand, representing power over life and death, and in his left hand, a globe, signifying his ability to carry out the divine plan. The Emperor is a capable leader and the Fool learns to ground these energies within himself.

The energy of this card brings you structure and stability. You are learning the importance of restrictions in parts of your life where you had previously not appreciated them. You are looking to develop discipline and perhaps some rules and routine could help you focus your efforts into a more purposeful way of being.

V. THE HIEROPHANT.

The Fool meets the Hierophant, a religious authority dressed in a red and white robe. His crown is gold and triple tiered. This is a community leader, possibly a spiritual teacher or counselor. He is giving his blessings while being watched by two kneeling monks.

This card teaches you to be part of a group. This may be a religious order or simply a social group that has helpful beliefs and values which you choose to adopt. You begin to enjoy the culture of this group and find your place in the world.

VI. THE LOVERS.

Archangel Raphael, the angel of Healing, blesses the two naked Lovers in the garden of Eden. The snake moves up the apple tree behind the woman and there is a burning tree behind the man. Behind them is a mountain with a high peak.

This is a card of healing and being in relationships with others. It is also a card of making a major choice. You are now considering the role of close relationships, intimate or otherwise, in your life. How will you accommodate these? What are your beliefs about relationships? What are your values?

VII. THE CHARIOT.

A Charioteer is seen here holding a wand in his right hand. He is well decorated and wears a crown on his head. There is a curtain of stars behind him and his chariot is led by two sphinxes of opposite color schemes which appear to be moving in two different directions. They represent the positive and negative forces. Although they are facing opposite directions, they seem to be held together by sheer will and determination. The chariot has two large wheels in water, receiving energy from the unconscious.

This could be a time when one must gather opposing or different resources and make them work together to proceed with strength and confidence. You are in touch with your inner conflicts and are called to listen to the needs behind each of them and harness the strength that polarity can offer when brought into conscious awareness. You are in control of yourself and have the conviction necessary to succeed.

VIII. STRENGTH.

This card shows a woman dressed in white holding the jaws of a lion. The lion and the woman seem to have a good relationship with each other and the lion willingly allows her to open its jaw. Its tail is between its legs showing that it has surrendered. She does not use force but tenderness and respect. Just like the Magician, she has the infinity symbol above her head. The Lion here represents our lower self, our fears and desires, our animal nature that keeps us in bondage and suffering. The Fool now learns to gather his own inner strength and gain momentum in his inner world.

This is a time to use gentle force. You could have a sense of courage that comes effortlessly to you even though to an onlooker it may look like an impressive feat that you are accomplishing. Unlike the assertive nature of the Charioteer, this card calls for a soft, loving approach to navigate the situation.

IX. THE HERMIT.

The lone elder man in a grey hooded cloak stands with a lantern in his right hand and a yellow walking stick in his left. Upon closer inspection the light in the lantern appears to be a star. There are minimal colors in this card, shades of grey, white and yellow. The Fool now seeks solitude and looks to his own inner guidance.

When the hermit appears, you are looking forward to a time of solitude and self-reflection. This card shows wisdom and self-referencing, a time to retreat into one's own depths and be led by one's own light. You have reached a significant part of your journey and have gathered much experience; it is now time to look within and carry on, perhaps leaving a few things behind. This is not a time to stop a project but perhaps to walk alone and guide oneself. The hermit is also sought by others to answer queries and provide guidance. The hermit depicted in the card looks down, as if in surrender to the light to guide his path. This star is your own inner light, which is now strong and able to lead the way. "Lead, kindly light."

X. WHEEL OF FORTUNE.

The Wheel of Fortune is a card of cycles. It signifies a change for the better. The Fool is met with good luck and is transitioning into a new cycle.

After the soul searching you experienced in the Hermit's card, you are ready for a change. There is perhaps something out of the ordinary appearing in your life, a chance encounter or a miracle that leads to a turning point in your journey. You appreciate how connected you are to the Whole and can see the patterns and cycles of life. This card changes the pace of things from slow to fast, if only for a while.

XI. JUSTICE.

The Juror holds the Sword of Justice in her right hand and the scales, representing balance, in her left. One white shoe is extended, showing readiness for action and purity of intention. The red robe signifies courage and desire.

When you see this card in a reading, you are becoming more aware of your part in the Whole and beginning to take responsibility for yourself. You know that your actions affect others and you are ready to own up your deeds and start anew. You are becoming more honest and that will reflect in your outer circumstances in time.

XII. THE HANGED MAN.

A man hangs upside down from a tree with his legs shaped like the number four. His hands are behind him and his hair hangs downward. There is a glowing halo around his head signifying divine guidance and inspiration. He is dressed in red and blue.

This card signifies surrender, letting go of the need to be right. You are being called to look at the situation from another perspective, perhaps the opposite of the one you have now. At first this may not be easy to do but some circumstances push us to the wall, and when you release the struggle, you'll be surprised by how things fall into place. This requires a new level of openness, trust and vulnerability. When you practice this, things look as though they are just as they should be.

XIII. DEATH.

Death comes riding a white horse and holding a black and white flag, symbolizing paradox. A man lies seemingly dead on the ground, and two young children kneel on the ground, one curious and the other looking away. A clergyman welcomes death with his hands in prayer. In the distance the sun rises between two towers.

This card reminds us of impermanence. You are ready to let go of that which does not serve you anymore. You can eliminate things from your life that do not represent who you are now, and this can free up a lot of life force energy you can use to move forward. You can do this consciously, or you can do it unwillingly, which will bring its own suffering. As you let things die in their own time, know that this is for the greater good and better days are sure to come.

XIV. TEMPERENCE.

With one foot on land and one foot in water, we see Archangel Michael pouring water from one cup into another. There is a winding path behind him that leads to the mountains and the sun is rising above them.

This is the card of moderation. After a long and tumultuous journey, you have learned to balance your emotions. You find ease in your days and begin to enjoy a sense of well-being and order. You are beginning to lead a harmonious life.

XV. THE DEVIL.

A man and a woman stand with chains loosely hanging around their necks. The Devil stands above them with a horned head and eagle legs, holding a lit torch. The backdrop is black.

This is the card of fear and ignorance. You are chained by some negative influences in your life. Perhaps you are aware of the damage of these self-imposed limitations, but like the couple on the card that can easily free themselves, you seem to be complacent in your comfort zone. Stretch out a little and let those addictions, negative thinking or temptations go. Once you overcome these, you will have access to a more fulfilling life.

XVI. THE TOWER.

A lightning bolt from the heavens hits the roof of a tower, setting it on fire. The bolt appears from an unknown source, representing the hand of the divine. The crown of the tower is falling and so are a man and a woman. There are flames coming out of the windows. The woman still has her crown on as she falls.

This card indicates a sudden change or catastrophe. Something big needed to shake up old patterns and limiting beliefs. This leads to a burning away of your ego. Any attitudes and behaviors that do not serve your higher self are sure to be lost in the crumbling of the tower. You may have been sitting in a comfortable place, not willing to acknowledge the invisible shackles you were bound by, so view this shattering in a positive way and you will find that this situation is a blessing in disguise.

XVII. THE STAR.

The Fool now encounters the Star. A naked woman, symbolizing a being of truth, is seen here kneeling on one knee by a body of water. She pours water out of the two pitchers in either hand, one into the water and the other onto the earth. It forms five streams when it reaches the ground. She gazes into the pool, perhaps engaging in self-reflection.

This is a time of inspiration. Perhaps you are about to attain something you have wished for. You are charged with a healing energy that soothes not just you but those around you as well. You feel a deep connection with the earth and all beings, and your heart is wide open to share and to love. You have returned from the underworld with some precious lessons and are now free to share your gifts with others. You are truly at peace now.

XVIII. THE MOON.

A dog and a wolf appear to be looking at the full moon, while a crustacean emerges from the water. In the background there are mountains, and in the foreground, a pool of water.

The Moon brings out things from deep within the unconscious. You may be riding a high and are charged with positive feelings but watch out for distortions of the truth. While your imagination is free and wild now, be sure to do a reality check occasionally. Stay close to your emotions but make no decisions just yet. "Sleep on it" is sound advice when you see this card in a reading.

XIX. THE SUN.

A large sun shines brightly in the sky. Below, sunflowers are in full bloom and a young naked child with golden hair is seen with arms open wide, sitting on a grey horse. The colors yellow, orange and sky-blue are prominent in this card.

The Sun card signifies warmth and joy like that of a sunny day after a series of cloudy and dark days. The naked child indicates that you are free in your spirit and have nothing to hide from others. You are looking forward to a good day or days and your joy and openness is well deserved. You radiate positive energy and draw in good feelings from those around you as you are in a place to share your own light and joy with them. There is a sense of lightheartedness and play in your surroundings and you are in the right place for success and accomplishment in your undertakings now. This could also be an indication of a sense of rebirth, a new beginning, a change of season and fresh energy.

XX. JUDGEMENT.

Archangel Gabriel appears in the heavens blowing a trumpet, signifying the channeling of a message from the divine. People below rise from their coffins, floating over water, welcoming imminent news or a verdict from the heavens. Here the Fool finally comes to know his own higher calling as he forgives himself and starts anew.

"May the most benevolent outcome arise out of our deeds."

A great journey is coming to fruition and you will soon hear news of where you have arrived after your diligent work. Judgement does not have a doomsday quality but that of a willing surrender to the highest good, better than perhaps what one's own imagination desires. This is a card of good will, a community card, that seeks the best for all, not just one. This is also a time to let go of the past and forgive yourself and those around you. A new day is here.

XXI. THE WORLD.

The World is the final card in the Major Arcana of the tarot. The naked cosmic dancing woman with a sash flowing around her body floats in grace, holding a baton in each hand. She is surrounded by a green wreath with red ribbons. On the four edges of this card are four heads: the cherub, the eagle, the bull and the lion.

"In the ocean of the world one only was, is and will be. You have neither bondage nor liberation. Live contented and be happy." - Ashtavakra Gita

When you get this card in a reading, you have mastered your physical, emotional or spiritual life in some way. It signifies the successful ending of a phase, life lesson, relationship or career and the edge of a new life. You may be coming to realize something of great significance for yourself and this inner knowing brings you a deep sense of fulfilment and peace. The great questions you had sought out in the beginning of the Fool's journey have been answered, and unlike the Fool, who is joyful but naive, your contentment comes from wisdom. You look to the World, the gates you have passed through, and reflect upon that which has been revealed. In this phase you are called to celebrate your achievements and acknowledge the immensity of the work you have carried out before you approach your next mission.

Yes, this also marks the beginning of a new mission, be it in your personal growth, your career or a relationship. This card asks you to harvest the freedom you have gained, so that before you move forward, you have finished the work in this realm. You are now in a position to serve the World with the gifts that you have received from the journey you've undertaken. The World recognizes you and looks to you for your knowledge, insight and guidance as one who knows. Answer this call and share your good harvest.

Chapter 5
Card Interpretations - The Minor Arcana

The Minor Arcana are the set of cards in the tarot that deal with the ordinary or mundane details of life and provide you with nuance in a reading. These cards are divided into four suits: Swords, Wands, Cups and Pentacles. Each of these suits has fourteen cards numbered Ace to ten and four court cards depicting royalty.

Swords

The suit of swords represents the element of air and governs the intellect, belief systems, thinking, perception and decision making. In the human body, this would be concerned with what lies above the neck - the mind in the traditional sense of the word. There is a misconception that the suit of swords always indicates struggle and fear, as the cards deal with some of the more difficult areas in the Minor Arcana. But we must keep in mind that challenges can be stepping stones to growth if we choose to take the opportunities they present to us, and the swords have the energy to cut through difficulty and come out clear on the other side.

Ace of Swords

A hand appears midair from a cloud, holding a decorated sword upright. The top of the sword has a crown and a wreath. There is a mountain range in the backdrop.

This card indicates new visions and ideas streaming into your thoughts. It brings the gift of absolute clarity and the energy to empower the mind. The rugged mountain range suggests that there are challenges ahead, but you can see them clearly and prepare wisely. The landscape is perceived correctly, and your vision is sharp and precise. This is a time to cut through any clouding of the mind through meditation and stillness. Keep your mind space free and let it be your wise witness.

Two of Swords

A woman sits blindfolded with crossed arms, holding two swords upright. There is water behind her with rocks jutting out. There are hills in the distance and the crescent moon shines above in the evening sky.

This is a card for decision making. There are two or more possibilities and perhaps an inability to see something about the situation is posing a challenge to you. You may be in a difficult situation, requiring some intellectual processing. Are you avoiding seeing the whole picture? What information do you need? What are you not looking at? You are still in a position of strength and clarity as suggested by the posture of the person sitting here. Take the time to weigh your options with care.

Three of Swords

The card depicts three swords pierced through a heart. There are dark clouds looming above and energy moving downwards in the grey backdrop.

This is a card of pain and grief. The heartache has already happened. You are carrying some sadness or pain. Others close to you may have been involved in this situation. Perhaps your expectations or thoughts have contributed to this heartache. You are encouraged to learn from this painful experience. Accept the wounding, pour your grief out in a safe way, and release the pain so you can move on.

Four of Swords

A man rests with his hands in prayer, and three swords rest above him on the wall. A final sword rests horizontally below him. Behind him is the painted glass of a church.

Take a break; let the mind rest. This is a sign that you should retreat into stillness and allow for the recovery of the mind. Take time off from any excessive mental stimulation. Go inward into prayer or whatever helps you recover your inner clarity. Sometimes processing happens through sleep and dreaming. Nothing more needs to be done here. Rest and recover.

Five of Swords

A young man appears to be grinning as he holds on to three swords. Two others look away dejected and disappointed. Two swords lie on the ground. There is a sea, mountains in the far distance and grey jagged clouds in the sky.

There has been a battle or conflict of some sort. New boundaries have been established and one person is not in agreement with the others. People are standing around, a bit defensive. Where do you stand in this conflict? The conflict is not yet resolved, and it seems like the participants are taking a break. There may be temporary loss of friendships or companions. Knowing your true motivations will help you own your inner power, and that cannot be shaken up by temporary external gains and losses.

Six of Swords

A man wades a little boat through wavy waters as a woman and child sit quietly in front of him. Six swords stand upright in the front of the boat. The shore is seen in the distance.

This is a card of transitions. There has been a shift in your situation and there's a moving away. A journey or travel may be in the cards and you are being supported or are supporting someone else through a transition. You may not be in high spirits but are moving toward more promising grounds. You are encouraged to move through your own intuition and feelings to help you make a decision. Let this take its own time.

Seven of Swords

A man with a sly grin on his face appears to be stealing five swords as he sneaks away from the village. Two swords remain upright nearby, unguarded. In the distance, the people are gathered near a bonfire, unsuspecting of this thief.

This card shows that something is being hidden. Someone may not be revealing their true thoughts or intentions and is hoping to get away with it. The yellow in this card also brings lightness and humor to the situation, suggesting that the deed could be a prank. Depending on the reading, you may want to examine your position in this scene and from whom you desire more honesty.

Eight of Swords

A blindfolded woman stands with her arms tied up, one foot in water and the other on land. There are eight upright swords around her. There is a village on the hills behind her.

This card indicates a sense of victimhood or being bound by one's negative thoughts. The person in this situation is caught up in some old patterns or limiting self-beliefs and feels like there is no escape. If only you look around you will see that freedom is close by. Step back, widen your perspective and look at where your mind has put you in a place of weakness. Explore what you can release to free yourself.

Nine of Swords

A man sits on his bed covering his face and looking disturbed. He may have just woken up from a nightmare. Nine swords hang horizontally on the black wall above him. The picture on the left corner of his bed shows two people in a fight, one defeated by the other. His blanket is decorated by prints of red roses and astrological signs.

This card depicts disturbances and depression. Your thoughts or outer circumstances have caused you a lot of mental anguish. In a relationship reading, this card indicates that there may have been some conflict that has led you to isolate and worry. The more you worry, the more distress you will bring upon yourself. Examine what is bringing you anguish and work on rectifying the situation, lest you be caught in a negative cycle.

Ten of Swords

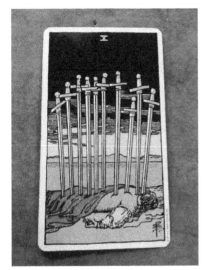

A man lies face down on the ground, bleeding, and seems to be dead. He has ten swords in his back that stand upright over his body. The sky above is dark but the sun rises on the horizon, bringing light into the scene. The sea below is calm and still.

The ten of swords signifies a painful ending. This could be the ending of a relationship, a career or a project that you did not see coming. This unexpected loss or betrayal deals a painful blow to you and you feel crushed under the weight of the pain. It is time to let go and surrender to the outcome of this situation. There is hope on the horizon and the prospects of emerging from this challenging situation in peace look promising. Wait and rest while the worst of it passes. Allow yourself to grieve and clear away the pain.

Page of Swords

A young man wields his sword in the air with both hands towards his left. He stands on a grassy knoll. In the distance there are large mountains. The sky is bright with fluffy clouds and a flock of ten birds flies away.

The page of swords brings signs of enthusiasm and curiosity. You have fresh ideas and are brimming with energy and zest. You have the passion to take up new plans and projects. The page is the archetype of learning and apprenticeship, but not mastery. Make sure to follow through with your plans if you want to see them take shape. This is a positive card for learning new ways of communicating or expressing yourself. Allow this energy to inspire you to do things you were putting off.

Knight of Swords

The knight charges ahead, leaning forward on his greyish white horse, ambitious and sure of where he wants to go. He raises his sword into the air with his right hand. The clouds above are jagged and a storm seems to be brewing. The knight is determinedly moving against the direction of the wind.

The knight of swords shows that you are determined and highly motivated. Nothing can stop you from going where you want to go, and you are willing to go against the grain to get your way. You are charged with energy and ambition and have the drive to move a long way swiftly. Keep in mind, you may not be considering the challenges ahead or weighing the consequences as you race forward. As long as you consider this, you are in a good place to meet your desires.

Queen of Swords

The queen of swords sits on a stone throne holding an upright sword in her right hand. Her left hand is raised as though delivering a verdict to her people. Her cape has a blue sky and white clouds printed on it. There is an angel and butterflies carved into her throne. Clouds gather in the sky behind her and there are trees blowing in the wind.

This card comes with a lot of confidence and mental clarity. The queen of swords has an inner strength that cannot be swayed by emotions. Perhaps you believe that emotions are not to be trusted while making fair decisions. You are straightforward and clear in your communication. You may not be the most empathic, but you can be trusted to see things rationally and judge things fairly. You are a clear thinker; you cut through fluff to deliver a fair verdict.

King of Swords

The king of swords sits on a tall stone throne wearing a blue tunic and holds a sword in his right hand. There are butterflies engraved on his throne. He sits on a grassy knoll. The air is still and the sky is fairly clear. Two birds fly in the distance.

The king of swords is the go-to authority for truth and clarity. If you are seeking advice from someone with a balanced perspective who also has a good deal of empathy, this is the kind of person you go to. You see things for what they are and you have compassion for others. You are rational in your approach. This is the person you go to for financial advice and matters that require the mind, not the emotions, to get the optimal result.

Wands

The suit of wands represents the element of fire. This is the energy of passion, determination, spirituality and intuition. Anything that you are passionate about or that drives you is represented by these cards. This transformative energy has the power to change things rapidly through force and willpower. It symbolizes the astrological signs of Leo, Sagittarius and Aries.

Ace of Wands

A white hand appears from a cloud midair, holding a wand with new leaves sprouting from it. There are mountains and a tall castle in the distance.

This card indicates that a new path or direction has appeared which has potential for growth and higher learning. If you were looking for a sign regarding whether you should take an opportunity, this card indicates that you should. Remember that the ace of wands, while promising, only indicates the possibility for success. It is up to you to pursue it if you so choose.

Two of Wands

A man holds a globe in one hand and the other rests on one of the two wooden poles beside him. The poles have new leaves sprouting from them. He seems to be standing on a terrace and looking into the distance. Below are grasslands with trees, houses and mountains, and a body of water in the distance.

The two of wands indicates that you are in a position to plan for the inspiration that came to you previously. You look over all that you have and consider the possibilities and where they may take you. You are not ready to act yet but are called to gather courage and resources for a decision that can have results reaching far into the future. You have the world in your hands, metaphorically speaking, and all you need is within you. Use your resources wisely.

Three of Wands

A man dressed in red and green robes stands between three tall wooden poles and rests his hand on the one on the far right. The poles have leaves sprouting from them. He looks toward the sea where the ships sail and there are mountains far away.

The three of wands indicates opportunities to reach out and expand into new areas of your life. Prospects for growth are appearing and you are ready and willing to take advantage of them. You are also looking at the challenges that lie ahead and preparing to meet them. You are in a position of comfort where you can look and see how vast the possibilities are. Adventure is in the cards.

Card Interpretations - The Minor Arcana

Four of Wands

Four decorated poles line the entrance to a scene of celebration. Two people wave flower bouquets in joy. There are other guests in the garden with them and we see their tall castle in the yellow backdrop.

The four of wands tells a tale of joy and merriment. There is reason to celebrate and you are encouraged to gather your family and loved ones to join you for a party or intimate gathering. You are called to see what's working well in your life and appreciate it. You have done good work; it is now time to celebrate the journey.

Five of Wands

Five young boys appear to be play fighting with five sticks, all sprouting new leaves at the top. They are dressed differently from each other, implying that none are on the same team, but each one is for himself. The competition among them is healthy and there seems to be camaraderie and mutual respect among the "fighters."

There may be small conflicts with others arising in your life, but the arguments are contained and proceed in a respectful way that may bring meaning and resolution that honors all parties. A higher degree of honesty is called for among one's own parts or among friends so you can see and hear each other more clearly and can sense each other's struggles in the group dynamic. You are being called to stand for and defend your position and not back down until a fair fight is put forward. This can also be a great time to practice and put to the test all the skills you have learned in the safety of a peer group and with the support of people who are rooting for each other while standing strong and true in their own power.

Six of Wands

A young man rides his horse, his head crowned with a victory wreath. He and several others who walk by his side hold tall staffs with leaves sprouting from them.

The six of wands indicates that you have succeeded in something you have been working on. This is a small win but a great pat on the back to let you know you are on the right track. You also win the recognition and praise of others around you, which adds to your confidence. While you keep your head firmly on your shoulders, go ahead and enjoy your time in the spotlight.

Seven of Wands

A young man holds a tall staff across his body to protect himself. Seven other staffs appear to be coming at him from below as he stands in defense. He wears two different shoes and stands on a grassy patch of land.

The seven of wands tells you that you need to take up your staff and protect yourself. There might be an attack that catches you off guard, as the mismatched pair of shoes imply, but you are standing on safe ground and this uprising is not yet a threat to you. Keep your guard up and don't let envy from those that may not be happy about your wins bring you down. If you are fighting to have your opinions or beliefs held up, be prepared for criticism and back your stance with reason. Maintain firm and healthy boundaries.

Eight of Wands

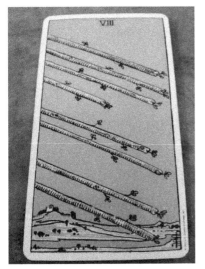

Eight wands fly through the sky. Each has new leaves sprouting from it and they all move in the same direction. There are grasslands and a river in the distance.

The eight of wands brings good news of change, movement and perhaps even air travel. There is a lot of energy for action in the cards and change in this situation can be fast moving and impactful. There is a lot of space in the landscape and nothing in your way, so take advantage of this potential and let the flow take you where you need to go.

Nine of Wands

An injured man holds his wand while he looks back cautiously at the eight other upright wands behind him. In the background are grassy hills.

The nine of wands shows that you have been through quite a journey and have been bruised by the travails. The finish line is near, and you watch carefully as you plan your next move. This is not the time to quit and although the battle isn't over yet, you are nearly done, and ease and success await you on the other side.

Ten of Wands

A blond man walks bent forward, clutching ten wands to himself. The weight is heavy, but he has a short way to go to reach his home.

The ten of wands shows that you are carrying a lot of responsibility that is weighing you down. You have slowed down in order to bear the weight, but you are positive that the end is near and you will soon be able to put down your burdens and rest. Your hard work will pay off, but for now you are walking the last mile to the finish line.

Page of Wands

A young man dressed in yellow stands on barren land keenly examining the leaves on a tall wand. There are yellow hills in the background.

The page of wands shows that you can find inspiration anywhere if you just look. You have the curiosity and imagination required to make something good out of a situation. You may not be in the best place resource-wise, but with your passion and determination you can create something of meaning with what you have. Although you possess these qualities, you haven't put them into action yet and you are still examining the prospects. Keep your mind open and you are likely to find the next steps to act upon.

Knight of Wands

The knight rides his brown horse forward as he holds his wand in his right hand. His yellow vest has lizard prints on it. The landscape is barren and there are mountains in the distance.

The knight of wands is high on passion. You are ready to start the projects you have been preparing for. You possess the courage and will to get this show on the road. You have plenty of room for growth and expansion, and even though there may be challenges on the horizon, you can see clearly and have the right attitude for success. If you are embarking on a new adventure, all the signs say go forth; you are ready!

Queen of Wands

The queen sits on her throne, flanked by lions carved into the stone. She holds her wand in her right hand and a sunflower in her left. Her robes are yellow and so are the mountains in the backdrop. A black cat sits at her feet.

The queen of wands is the epitome of confidence. You are in a social mood and can carry yourself well. You are popular and known for your elegance. You carry the energy of Leo, the fire sign of the zodiac, and can be quick-witted and intense. That said, you have full control over your fiery energy and passion and are in touch with your shadows as well. You are ready to own your power and shine bright socially. There is nothing to hide now; you are your own master.

King of Wands

The king sits on his yellow throne dressed in red, green and yellow. His cape and his throne have lizard designs on them and there is a lizard on the ground near him.

The king of wands is the card of the true visionary. You are full of fire energy, and you know how to tend it. You have reached a level of mastery with your power and are capable of leading others toward a common vision. You are an attractive leader and do not need to do much to gather a loyal following to support your vision. This is the card of revolutionaries. Focus on keeping your intentions pure and you will make a difference through the positive changes that you aspire to bring.

Cups

The suit of cups represents the element of water and the realm of emotions, feelings and relationships. Some of the cards are associated with romantic relationships, family, community, nature, and your emotional connection with yourself. They also stand for balance and connection between the inner and outer worlds. In astrology, the cups represent the signs of Pisces, Cancer and Scorpio.

Ace of Cups

A hand appears from a cloud in the sky, holding a golden chalice inscribed with an upside down M. Five streams of water fall from it into the water below, where pink lilies float. A white dove flies down into the cup, inserting a coin with a cross into it.

The ace of cups signifies new beginnings. It is a sign of new relationships and connections, and an indication that relationships are in good health. There is also a sense that a divine hand is adding a gift, a token of support into one's emotional life. The streams show good health and flow. Remember to welcome the new opportunity.

Two of Cups

A man and a woman raise their cups to each other, and the man reaches over to touch the woman's cup. A winged lion's head, known as Caduceus, hovers above them with a staff and two intertwining serpents below. In yogic tradition, the two serpents represent Ida and Pingala, the yin and yang forces respectively.

This is a card of friendship and shared connection and understanding. It's associated with relationships based on mutual trust and respect, and perhaps indicates that two people work well together. In a work-related reading, this could indicate that you are connecting well with a colleague and you have a healthy working relationship. In the case of a love reading, perhaps you are experiencing the beginning stages of mutual attraction and a romantic connection. In other readings, this card can indicate healthy communication and emotional satisfaction.

Three of Cups

Three well-dressed young women move in a circle raising their cups to each other in celebration. Their robes are white, red and yellow, signifying purity, passion, happiness and friendship. The garden is full of ripe fruit.

The three of cups is a community card, that of close friends, allies and supporters. It depicts what looks like a party or an intimate gathering of friends. It indicates that you have people around you who are happy for you and take joy in your successes. It is also a card of sisterhood, and represents camaraderie and shared values.

Four of Cups

The card shows a young man sitting under a tree with his arms crossed. Three cups sit in front of him and a fourth appears to be offered to him by a mystery hand coming out of a cloud. The man is not looking at this offering, nor does he look at the three cups in front of him. His eyes are turned down, and he is perhaps looking inward.

The appearance of this card signifies a time of inner contemplation and meditation. This may be a time of withdrawing into oneself, perhaps even turning down new opportunities or invitations. There is a sense of temporarily stopping activities to gain a better understanding of what you need to feel a sense of accomplishment or purpose. You may need time to consider what you already have before accepting new opportunities.

Five of Cups

A man in a black cloak looks down sorrowfully at three fallen cups, from which red and green liquid has spilled. Two cups are still standing behind him. Ahead, there is a river and a bridge that connects to the other side, where there is a home and greenery. The sky is gray.

The five of cups signifies loss and mourning. Perhaps you have lost a loved one or an important relationship is endangered. There are hurt feelings and regret, and you may be overlooking what is still going well in your life. It is a reminder that while it is important to grieve, you must count your blessings as well. The loss has probably led to isolation or withdrawal from home or community; when you are ready, you can cross over to go back home.

Six of Cups

A young boy smells a white daffodil in a cup as he passes it to a younger girl. Each cup has a daffodil growing out of it. They stand on the yellow lawn of a yellow house. A man walks toward the house in the distance holding a walking stick. The sky above is clear. The yellow and white in the picture signifies purity, joy and friendship.

The six of cups is a card about childhood and memories. A soft innocence comes through this card. You are probably remembering things from early life, perhaps involving siblings or playmates from a time gone by. In a reading, this card can point to something from your childhood that can provide answers to a current scenario or indicate that someone or something from the past will appear in your life again.

Seven of Cups

Seven cups appear in a cloud presenting different things to a man: a person's head, a person with open arms shrouded by a blanket, a snake, a castle over a hill, jewels, a victory wreath, and a dragon. The silhouette of the man faces them with a raised arm.

The seven of cups calls attention to distractions and temptations. When this card appears in a reading, ask yourself what is motivating your intentions and actions. Is there something superficial promising short term gains that is drawing you away from your true goals? If so, this card advises you to hold a stronger awareness of your truth. This may be a time to step back and let these distractions pass until you can see more clearly.

Eight of Cups

Eight cups are neatly stacked in the foreground. Across the river, a man wearing a red coat and red boots walks away from the cups, supported by a walking stick. There are green hills in the distance and a waning crescent moon and a full moon in the sky.

The eight of cups is associated with relinquishing one's material accomplishments for spiritual pursuits. The scene depicts a man carefully leaving behind some things he once valued, but have perhaps brought disappointment or lack of fulfilment. You are ready for a spiritual journey to higher emotional ground.

Nine of Cups

A man dressed in white robes and a red turban sits on a wooden bench. He wears a smile and his arms are crossed over his chest. On a raised platform behind him, nine goblets are displayed. The curtain covering the platform is blue and the room is yellow.

The nine of cups signifies material prosperity. There is a sense of satisfaction and ease in the man's demeanor and he appears to be wealthy. Depending on where in the reading this card appears, you either want or are currently enjoying material success and luxury.

Ten of Cups

A man and woman stand together holding each other at the hip, each with one arm outstretched to the sky. Their children play beside them. A rainbow of red, green and yellow with ten golden cups appears in the sky. Their home is seen in the distance. The scene reflects happiness and peace.

The ten of cups is the card of ultimate happiness and joyful relationships. Compared to the nine of cups, this card has more to do with emotional than material success. While it may not depict much material wealth, it depicts a fulfilling life. You can expect to enjoy ease and love in your relationships.

Page of Cups

A young man dressed in blue and red holds a goblet in one hand with a blue fish jumping out of it. The pattern on his tunic is floral. He is standing by a wavy sea.

This card is associated with empathy and artistic abilities. You are in tune with your emotional world, even though you may not always be practical. It is a time of learning how to navigate watery emotions through feeling and sensing. Your creativity is flowing, and you're surprised by how skillfully you respond to new insights jumping at you from your unconscious. Channel your creativity and emotions into something you value.

Knight of Cups

An armored knight rides a grey horse, holding a goblet in his right hand. His helmet and footwear have wings on the back. His cape has red fish printed on it. The horse marches on and behind them there is a river, trees and hills.

The knight of cups is a passionate, charming person who brings a loving energy into the reading. This is a person who is romantic and creative. You are attractive to others and you genuinely care about the people around you. Your empathy is informed by your own depth of self-understanding and self-love. If you have a creative endeavor in mind, this is the time to make your dreams a reality.

Queen of Cups

A queen sits on her thrown on land, on what appears to be the bank of a flowing river. At her feet lie colorful pebbles and shells. She holds a closed and adorned trophy-like cup, which she examines carefully with both hands. Of all the cards in this suit, only the queen has a closed cup. Angels are carved into her stone throne.

The queen here signifies a caring and calm presence with a strong sense of inner knowing. She is in control of her emotional landscape and can see your motivations and those of others in a compassionate and centered manner. Your knowing comes from a deep place within. You could be a good healer, counselor or friend, and perhaps provide an emotionally stable environment for someone who needs support.

King of Cups

The king of cups sits steady on a stone throne in the middle of a sea. He holds a golden goblet in one hand and a scepter in the other. He is dressed in blue and yellow robes. A ship sails away behind him.

This card shows mastery over one's emotional world and intuition. When you are dealing with the king of cups, you have achieved a state of balance and steady calmness in your inner world. While things may appear rocky and ever-changing in your outer circumstances, you know yourself so well that you are able to handle these dramas with ease and grace. You are open to your emotions and those of others and are capable of balancing them with logic and reasoning. This is a leader who can be rational and empathic at the same time and deserves trust from others.

Pentacles

The suit of pentacles represents the earth element. It reveals information about our relationship with money, work, career, home and property. Everything related to our practical needs on the material plane are represented by the pentacles. This suit is connected to the signs of Taurus, Virgo and Capricorn.

Ace of Pentacles

A hand appears from a cloud presenting a large yellow coin or pentacle. In the background is a green orchard and mountains.

Whatever you are looking for is coming to you. This card indicates success with family, roots, career and finance. If it is a new career you are seeking, perhaps a job offer is on the way. Money from an unexpected source is also possible. If your concern regards home and property, good luck is coming to you. This is a positive sign that ensures grounding and earth energy. Your needs are fulfilled.

Two of Pentacles

A juggler in a red suit and orange vest juggles two pentacles in each hand, connected by a green infinity belt. He has one foot off the ground. Behind him are high seas and two sailing ships.

This is a card about balance. Perhaps you have two or more opportunities and you are contemplating which to take. Maybe you have a lot going on in your life and your hands are full. The card represents maintaining the right balance so that you can find stability and ease as you navigate the ups and downs of your situation. Everything is connected, so keep calm and ride the waves in a centered and equanimous way.

Three of Pentacles

A young stonesman stands on a wooden bench as he works on carving out the cathedral walls. The architects show him their plan and take his inputs.

This card speaks of collaboration. It is important to know that even if you are young and inexperienced, you have a lot to contribute to the team. This card foretells a situation in which two or more people are collaborating to make something work. It is a positive sign whether in a reading for a romantic relationship or a career. There is learning and growth for all involved in this project or area of concern. Carry on!

Four of Pentacles

A rich man wearing a crown is seated on a stone seat. He hugs a pentacle, while one rests on his crown and two lie beneath his feet. We see a prosperous town in the background.

This is a card of holding tight. You are holding something of value back and you do not want to share it with anyone. This may lead you to push people away and hide if necessary. You are sacrificing love for the sake of security. You might be holding valuable information about your life, thoughts and feelings close to your chest as a protective mechanism. Consider what you can loosen your hold on that will bring you more peace and connection with others.

Five of Pentacles

A poor man and woman tread through a snowy landscape. The man is disabled and is supported by crutches. They walk past a mosaic church window. It looks warm inside, but they are either not invited or do not feel the need to stop by.

This is a card about material or spiritual poverty. Perhaps you or someone you know is going through a hard time and dredging along with a heavy spirit. You may not be alone in this and there might be a sense of camaraderie in going through these challenges. Look for a spiritual or grounding resource to tend to your worries and nurse your wounds. A little tender loving care goes a long way in healing what is broken or aching.

Six of Pentacles

The man in the center of the card gives coins to a man who bows at his feet, as another man looks on and waits for his turn to receive. In his other hand, he holds the scales of justice.

In the material realm, this is a time to share. Depending on where you see yourself in this card, you are being called to give what you can or be open to receiving from someone who has something that can help you. This is a time for distribution of resources so that balance is restored, and opportunities are made available.

Seven of Pentacles

A man rests his chin on his hands which hold a shovel sticking in the mud. He has already planted his seeds and patiently watches the harvest grow on the vine.

This is a card about slow but sure payoff. You have sown some seeds and are being called to patiently watch as your work comes to fruition. As you wait, consider how you got to this position and what steps you can take to improve in the future. For now, patience is key. Remember to appreciate yourself for all the effort you put in.

Eight of Pentacles

A young craftsman etches a pentacle into stone. He has already etched seven pentacles which hang from the tree and lie next to him.

This is a card about apprenticeship and paving your way through diligent practice. It is a call to commit to practicing a skill you enjoy and honing it to mastery. Getting good at something takes time and effort. Attend to the details of your work or relationship and bring your focus and determination to seeing it through. You are on the right path and you have what it takes; now it's time to put in the work.

Nine of Pentacles

A woman dressed in rich yellow robes stands in a grapevine garden. In her left hand is a rare and beautiful bird. In the distance is a big country house and mountains.

This is a card about enjoying the finer things in life. You have a taste for expensive things and indulge in beauty and luxury. You are invited to appreciate what is rare and precious and notice that you are surrounded by delicate and lovely things. Practice gratitude for all that you have and cherish it.

Ten of Pentacles

This card depicts a happy scene with a young couple enjoying each other's company, a child beside the woman, and an elder patriarch watching over them as two dogs accompany him. The elder man's robes are decorated with grapevines. Their large house is behind them

This is the card of legacy. We see three generations of a family along with their pet friends. There is love between all of them and a commitment to each other. In a reading, this card promises good fortune in terms of family and relationships and shared resources that nourish all. The well-being of the whole is key to each of its members.

Page of Pentacles

A young man stands in a grassy field with flowers by his feet. He holds up a pentacle to his face, keenly examining it. We see a large mountain range in the distance.

This is a time to develop skills and improve your finances. The energy of this card is a keen and open spirit and the capacity to engage in what you are interested in pursuing. There may be challenges on the horizon, but if you see them as a growth opportunity, you can learn from them and improve your situation. If you want to start a new venture or project, the page inspires keen study and laying out good plans for the road ahead.

Knight of Pentacles

The armored knight sits on his tall, dark horse holding a pentacle. He looks at it patiently and is not in a hurry to go anywhere. Ahead of them is a tilled field being prepared for sowing season.

This card calls for slow and steady work. You are in this for the long run and are encouraged to use your wisdom and foresight to plan out your next steps. The work is hard, but long-term prospects are promising. Take one step at a time and watch out for the details of your process. Every little thing counts and will be accounted for. Patience and hard work are key.

Queen of Pentacles

The queen sits on a beautifully crafted stone throne in a garden of flowers. A rabbit runs across the right edge of the picture. She carefully holds a pentacle in her lap. There are roses growing above and around her.

This card represents nurturance and independence. You are in a position where you can care for your own material needs and desires and comfortably nourish others as well. You are sought by some in your life for the warmth and loving presence you provide. Think of the friend who always has something cooking in their kitchen when you arrive and seems to have a great work-life balance. That is the queen of pentacles.

King of Pentacles

The king sits on his throne with a wand in one hand and a pentacle in the other. He wears robes printed with grapevine. The bulls' heads on the top of his chair signify Taurus, the sign of earthly stability.

This card communicates that you have invested well, and your foresight has brought you material success and security. You not only can provide for your needs and the needs of others in the present, but also have laid a solid foundation to continue doing so in the future. Your discipline helps you stay on top of your financial situation, making you an able provider and reliable leader. You have made good choices and need only focus on the path you have chosen. You need not endure any more risks as you have all you need for a comfortable life.

Chapter 6
Tarot Spreads

Just like weaving together a good story, the tarot can tell you a little or a lot based on what you ask. Sometimes all you need is one answer to assess the situation. Other times you are looking for the twists in the plot, details on the main characters and how they interact with each other, where the blind spots are, and where the opportunities for fulfillment are. Spreads are templates you can use to weave a story. Each template will have positions for your cards that represent various pieces of the story. For instance, in a basic three-card spread with the past, present and future, the place each card falls tells that part of the story. If the Tower shows up in the past position, you may see that as a challenging period that has already passed, as opposed to it appearing in the present position in the reading

In Chapter 3, we practiced a one-card reading. Prior to all readings we should follow the preparatory exercise we described earlier.

Calling in and Letting go (two-card spread)

This is a wonderful spread to receive guidance on what you want more of in your life and what you need to let go of. Also known as the Invite and Release spread, this is a great way to journal about what energies, habits, patterns, and thoughts you are ready to bring in and what you are ready to clear out from your life.

Gifts and Growth Areas (two-card spread)

This spread helps you understand what your gifts and weaknesses are. Based on the readings, you can learn to work with your strengths and pay more attention to areas you are lacking in.

Past, Present, Likely Outcome (three-card spread)

This is one of the most well-known spreads. The card on the left shows the past situation, which influenced the card in the middle position (the present), and the card on the right (the future). I prefer to call the future card the 'likely outcomes" card. Getting a sense of the direction that the past and present positions are revealing, one can decide to continue towards this outcome or change something to elicit a more favorable outcome.

A Five-Card Spread

The first position shows us the present, the second shows the past, the third shows the likely outcome or advice, the fourth shows the unconscious and the fifth shows the promise or blessing in the situation. This is a great spread to get more details and tap into your unconscious drives, desires and expectations that you may be bringing to the situation in question.

Chapter 7
Creating your Tarot Space

It is important to have a good setting in which to do tarot readings. This includes both the internal and the external environment. To prepare internally, we set intentions and do awareness practices or short meditations before beginning our readings. And to support our internal state, a good external environment can be equally important. Here are some things to consider regarding your tarot space:

- Clean and free of clutter - Your tarot space does not need to be a large area. You only need enough room to sit comfortably and lay out your cards in front of you. Make sure you remove any objects that clutter up this space. You want to have a clear mind and clear view as you begin to read.

- Quiet - Choose a relatively quiet spot in your house to practice reading. Somewhere you will not be interrupted by people or sounds. This can help you go deep within and listen to your inner guidance.

- Sacred - You can create a small altar with a soothing color scheme for your tarot deck and line it with a cloth that feels good to you. You can place objects in the space that are special to you, like rocks or crystals. Images that help you connect to the divine or encourage a meditative state can be helpful. Play around with the elements and see if you can bring a representation of each element onto your altar. Remember that all of this is optional.

- Lighting - Play around with natural or soft lighting. Lighting has an effect on the mood of a space, so make it warm and welcoming for you and those you may read for.

- Music - Readers have varied opinions on this. Some people do not like playing music while reading. I like to play soft reiki music or healing frequency tracks. If you are in an environment where you cannot avoid loud external sounds, music can help soften the space and make it easier for you to relax.

- Candles and incense - These mood setters can help you create your desired ambiance. You can select different aromas for specific intentions and experiment until you find the ones that suit you best.

- For the traveling reader - Some of us travel a lot and like to carry our cards with us. Make sure to keep your cards in a safe case or pouch. You can make a cloth pouch with fabric that you like, to protect your cards from damage as you travel. You can also create a mini altar that you can set up anywhere. This not only provides a great setting for your readings away from home, but also brings you a sense of familiarity and grounding while on the move.

Get creative. Bring your essence and expression to the space, whether that means being minimal or decorative.

Chapter 8
Conclusion

We have arrived at the end of this course. Just as the nature of the suits, I hope you gather all your inner resources to make the best of your time with the tarot. This book covers the basics of reading the tarot. As you proceed you will start to develop a style and practice that is unique to you.

You may want to connect with others who love the tarot as much as you do. There are many resources you can tap into for support on your journey ahead. Here are some that I have found most helpful:

Online Tarot Websites and Communities

There are many popular websites that share tarot-related teachings, news and reviews. Some have online forums where you can post your questions and they will be answered by fellow tarot readers from across the world. You can also start reading for each other and take your practice to the next level. Websites like biddytarot.com, trustedtarot.com and littleredtarot.com offer courses and free member portals. Facebook groups like Tarot Nerds and Tarot Readers Academy are a great way to connect with people and learn from each other.

Metaphysical Stores

If you prefer meeting people in real life, you can ask the metaphysical stores in your region to help connect you with meetup groups or local resources.

Trusted Friends and Family

Once you decide to start reading for others, you can introduce friends and family that you trust to this part of your world. Stay open to feedback you receive from them. Take what feels right for you and leave aside what does not resonate. This is a big step in becoming known as a tarot reader. Some of us may breeze through this part and others may be reluctant. Be gentle with yourself and follow your own inner guidance.

However your journey with the tarot emerges, I hope you cherish it and find great comfort and companionship in it, and that it brings you what you need. This is only the beginning; many exciting possibilities await you. Enjoy every bit of it. Good luck!

If you enjoyed this book as much as I've enjoyed writing it, you can subscribe* to my email list for exclusive content and sneak peaks of my future books.

Visit the link below:

http://eepurl.com/duVEgf

OR

Use the QR Code:

(*Must be 13 years or older to subscribe)

CPSIA information can be obtained
at www.ICGtesting.com
Printed in the USA
BVHW031948311021
620410BV00006B/319